MANAGING YOUR
MONEY AND FINANCES™

Buying
Your First
Car

Xina M. Uhl and Daniel E. Harmon

Rosen
YA™

New York

Published in 2020 by The Rosen Publishing Group, Inc.
29 East 21st Street, New York, NY 10010

Copyright © 2020 by The Rosen Publishing Group, Inc.

First Edition

Library of Congress Cataloging-in-Publication Data

Names: Uhl, Xina M., author. | Harmon, Daniel E., author.
Title: Buying your first car / Xina M. Uhl and Daniel E. Harmon.
Description: First edition. | New York : Rosen Publishing, 2020.
| Series: Managing your money and finances | Audience: Grades
7–12. | Includes bibliographical references and index.
Identifiers: LCCN 2018048115| ISBN 9781508188469
(library bound) | ISBN 9781508188452 (paperback)
Subjects: LCSH: Automobiles—Purchasing. | Consumer education.
Classification: LCC TL162 .U35 2020 | DDC 629.222029—dc23
LC record available at https://lccn.loc.gov/2018048115

Manufactured in the United States of America

CONTENTS

INTRODUCTION

There's no two ways about it. Americans love their cars. In fact, huge parts of the country developed after the beginning of the automobile age in the early twentieth century. The coming of the automobile changed how Americans lived and worked. Roads, cities, and towns were built on the assumption that the residents would use cars to get around. Older, more compact cities had a walkable core area, where it was possible for a person to walk to his or her grocer, house of worship, school, and workplace. Mass transit in the form of streetcars and trains extended the distance that people could travel with ease. But the coming of the automobile extended that reach even farther, and roads, suburbs, and workplaces were constructed with this in mind.

In time, the automobile became associated with the American way of life: baseball, apple pie, and cars.

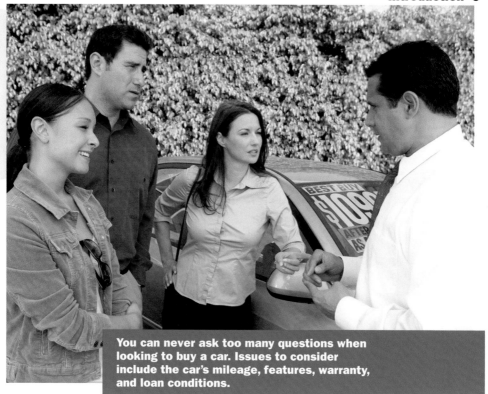

You can never ask too many questions when looking to buy a car. Issues to consider include the car's mileage, features, warranty, and loan conditions.

The costs of vehicle ownership have only grown over the years. Data from the Federal Reserve Bank of New York show that in 2017 consumers took out $568.6 billion in loans to purchase cars—the highest amount ever.

You may not have thought much about how expensive cars are. The sticker price doesn't tell the whole picture. Driving it regularly results in ongoing costs for fuel. Maintenance must be done on a schedule to keep the vehicle running well. Repairs crop up unexpectedly as parts wear out, such as the exhaust system or the brakes. You will need new tires every 20,000 to 40,000 miles (32,186 to 64,372 kilometers). You must pay taxes on the car to your local government each year. An insurance policy is a must, too—one that comes with high costs in your teen and young adult years. Insurance may cover the costs of serious accidents or damage, but you probably will have to pay part of the repair costs. Because of all the expenses involved, some people cannot afford a car. Teens often need help from their parents to buy their first car, even if they save most of their earnings from a part-time job for several years. Whether or not you have help from your parents, you should examine the costs of a car very carefully before investing in one. Not only must you pay the purchase price of the car, but you must also earn enough to keep the car going.

Perhaps, after carefully preparing and examining a car budget, you may decide that the overall cost is not worth it. Maybe you want a car more than you need one. You may decide to wait to buy one until you are out of high school or college and have a full-time job. When you decide it's time for your first car, a thoughtfully prepared, honest car cost worksheet will reveal what kind of vehicle you can (or can't) afford. The pages ahead will give you a true picture of everything involved in purchasing a vehicle so that you can make the most of your money.

CHAPTER ONE

The Costs
of Cars

Making the decision to buy your first car can make for an exciting time. You may already have picked out a red sports car or a pickup truck with giant wheels. Maybe you are still looking for the perfect car. You've started to pay attention to car ads and banners at automobile dealerships or used car lots. Friends, relatives, and neighbors may have cars to sell. It's time to learn all you can about this big step in life.

Many of the deals you see seem incredible. If you're a teenager with income from a part-time job and you understand the basics about budgeting and "smart money," then it may seem that you surely can afford to buy a car—now.

Maybe you can. Read beyond the advertisements, though. A young car buyer must itemize all the costs that will be involved. The advertised (purchase) price is just the beginning.

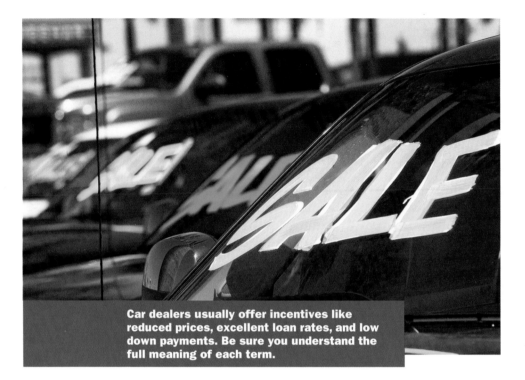

Car dealers usually offer incentives like reduced prices, excellent loan rates, and low down payments. Be sure you understand the full meaning of each term.

A Car's Real Price

You will find more than one descriptive pricing sticker on the window of a new car. A used car may carry one or more. The numbers are different. Why?

The invoice price is the amount that the auto manufacturer charges the auto dealer. In order to make money, the car dealer must charge the customer more than this. The invoice price is basically just for your information.

The Monroney sticker is the information sheet that federal law requires to be displayed on a window of every new vehicle sold in the United States. (It isn't required on used vehicles.) It lists the car's or truck's standard and optional equipment, engine and transmission types, and estimated gas mileage (or kilometrage). (Mileage,

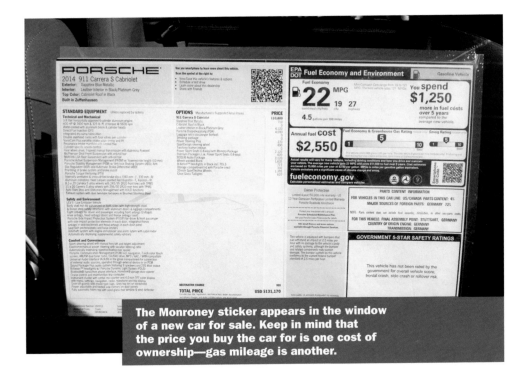

The Monroney sticker appears in the window of a new car for sale. Keep in mind that the price you buy the car for is one cost of ownership—gas mileage is another.

or fuel economy, estimates are rated by the Environmental Protection Agency, or EPA.) The sticker shows the manufacturer's suggested retail price (often noted as the MSRP) and the cost of each optional feature. It also provides warranty information.

The auto dealer attaches a separate window sticker below or beside the Monroney sticker. This is the actual price that the dealer is asking for the car. It usually is higher than the MSRP because it includes extras the dealer has provided, such as paint protection. In most cases, you can get the seller to lower the advertised price of the car.

While you consider the various stickers, you might find yourself overwhelmed by quick-sell marketing techniques. Auto dealers have always been regarded as high-pressure salespeople. Many dealers offer what appear to be unbelievable terms. Some

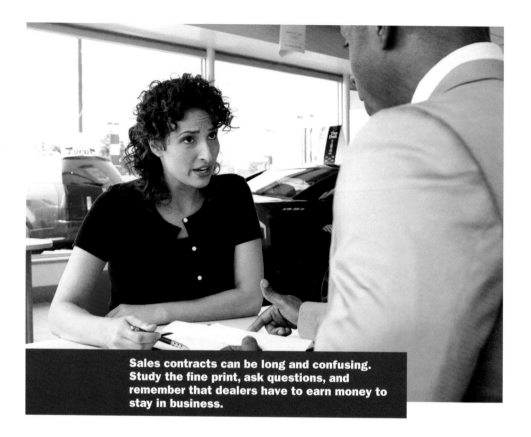

Sales contracts can be long and confusing. Study the fine print, ask questions, and remember that dealers have to earn money to stay in business.

examples are no down payment, no monthly payments for six months or a year, and no problems with customers' bad credit histories.

You are led to believe that you can walk into the dealership with no money at all in your pockets, drive out in a nice (possibly brand-new) car, and pay nothing for a long time to come. Just remember the old saying, "If it seems too good to be true, then it probably is." What those dealers don't reveal until you sit down with them to talk terms is that, sooner or later, you're going to have to pay in full—and then some. Once you begin making payments, you'll likely end up paying more for the car than you would have under less fantastic but more sensible circumstances.

To begin with, they are offering only certain cars under those delayed-payment terms. In many cases, you do need a good credit record in order to qualify. Your interest rate for the car loan may be much higher than you expect (or can get if you shop around). Overall, the terms may be far less desirable than the terms that you can easily find elsewhere. For example, the seller might require you to buy an extended service contract or special features.

Insurance Comparison

Auto insurance companies offer policies with a confusing array of terms and prices. Some cover almost every eventuality. Others cover only the basics; when an accident occurs, the insurers look for ways to avoid paying. Most policies require the owner to pay a deductible for damages. That means the car owner must directly pay a certain amount—usually, the first few hundred dollars—for any repair. Only then does the insurer take over the costs.

Shopping for the best auto insurance policy is an ongoing challenge for drivers. You should review and compare your coverage every few years.

Always remember that car dealers have to earn a living. They have no cars to give away, and they cannot sell them to you for less than they paid for them.

Taxes and More

Sales tax on a car is based on your state or county's tax structure. If you buy a $20,000 car and the sales tax in your area is 5 percent, then that will be an extra $1,000 ($20,000 x .05 = $1,000). It's just the beginning of taxes that you will have to pay over time. Your car will be taxable property for as long as you own it. Property taxes on a car can amount to $500 or more each year. Taxes go down from year to year as the car's value decreases. Bear in mind, though, that sales and property taxes eventually add up to thousands of dollars.

Most states require car owners to buy auto insurance. The two main types of car insurance are collision and liability. Collision insurance covers damages to your car caused by your own error. Liability insurance pays others who are victims of your driving mistakes. It includes vehicle damage and medical costs.

Some states require a driver to have only liability insurance in order to obtain a driver's license.

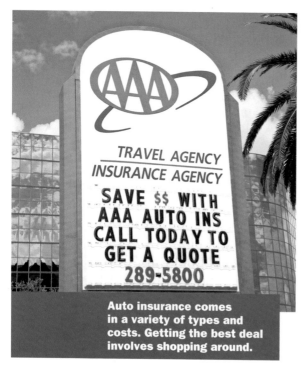

Auto insurance comes in a variety of types and costs. Getting the best deal involves shopping around.

According to most advisers, you really need more insurance than that. You can also buy comprehensive coverage (to include theft and damage by fire, vandalism, and other causes) and uninsured motorist protection. The latter will help fix your car if it is damaged by a driver who has no insurance.

Young drivers generally must pay much more for auto insurance than older drivers because statistics show that they're involved in more accidents. In some states, teenage drivers can get lower insurance rates if they pass driver-training courses. If they are charged with a traffic violation or they cause an accident, then their insurance rates will most likely increase.

The car dealer may add post-sale fees for performing tasks like inspecting the vehicle, filing paperwork with the highway department, and "protecting" the paint job with a rust-proof coating. Ask for explanations of every sales detail before you sign a purchase agreement.

Those are the immediate costs of buying a car. There will be ongoing costs. Besides the monthly payments and upkeep expenses, unexpected repairs are inevitable. And a sad reality is that your car begins to lose value the moment you sign the papers and drive off in it.

Myths and Facts

Myth The least expensive car is the best deal. When it starts to have serious problems, just trade it for another cheap car.

Fact That cheap car may get poor fuel efficiency and may require more frequent and more expensive routine maintenance. It may cost more to insure. Its resale value will be less than that of a more reliable car.

Myth Distance driven is the most important factor to consider when buying a used car. The less distance driven, the better.

Fact Distance driven is an important indicator, but it's not necessarily the most important. Pre-owned vehicles that have been driven responsibly for about 120,000 miles (about 200,000 km) may be capable of running another 100,000 miles (about 160,000 km) or more without needing major repairs. Any car that has been damaged or driven abusively can be a very bad deal.

Myth If the dealer reduces the price to only a few hundred dollars "above invoice," then I'm getting a terrific deal.

Fact In some situations, it might be a great deal but not always. There are reasons why the dealer is willing to sell the car at a low markup. The model may be selling poorly or is about to be discontinued. It may have a poor maintenance record. The dealer may receive a rebate amounting to thousands of dollars from the automaker after the sale.

CHAPTER TWO

Finding Your Best First Car

A fter looking at all the costs associated with car ownership, you may decide that you have enough cash to take the plunge. Whatever way you look at it, cars cost money, both up front when you buy them and ongoing due to fuel and maintenance costs. Now, though, you have a realistic idea of what you are getting yourself into.

Now, it's time to go shopping. You might start by visiting the Consumer Reports website (http://www.consumerreports .org). It reports details about specific vehicles. It also publishes comparisons and calculations on the cost, over time, of owning certain vehicles.

The Council of Better Business Bureaus website (http://www .bbb.org) is another good resource. You can find tips on buying cars online, buying new and used cars, buying car insurance, service contracts, and more.

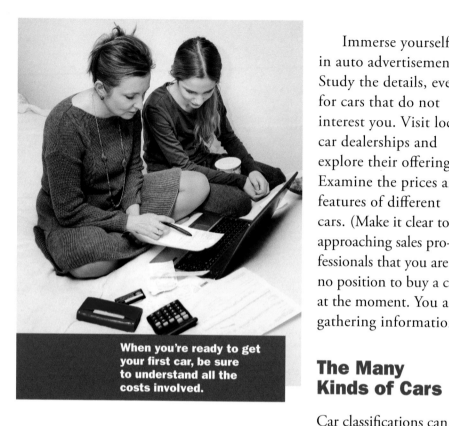

When you're ready to get your first car, be sure to understand all the costs involved.

Immerse yourself in auto advertisements. Study the details, even for cars that do not interest you. Visit local car dealerships and explore their offerings. Examine the prices and features of different cars. (Make it clear to approaching sales professionals that you are in no position to buy a car at the moment. You are gathering information.)

The Many Kinds of Cars

Car classifications can be confusing. There are minicars, superminis, subcompacts, compacts, and "family cars." You can investigate cabriolets, hatchbacks, sports cars, sedans, station wagons, multipurpose vehicles (MPVs), and sport utility vehicles (SUVs). You should look at all of them and decide which will best suit your purposes. What do you need for transportation? Where do you frequently go? Do you often travel with others? How many at a time?

For most teenage car buyers, a compact car or small family car works nicely. But while compact economical cars clearly are practical, certain factors may lead you to buy a very different vehicle type. Some parents want their teen children to drive

While sports cars like this may look good and have lots of power, they are seldom the best choice for a first car.

SUVs, for example, because drivers of those cars generally are better protected in collisions than drivers of compact cars. Safety is more important to them than fuel economy.

Fuel Costs Make a Difference

The sales sticker on the window will indicate the new car's expected gas mileage (or kilometrage) for city and highway driving. Vehicles get less efficiency in city driving and heavy rush-hour traffic because of frequent starts and stops. It takes extra fuel each time you accelerate the car. On the open road, you can maintain a steady speed. Energy experts advise motorists to drive as if a delicate eggshell is beneath the accelerator pedal. Avoid crushing the eggshell because pressing the accelerator burns more gas.

Regular, mid-grade, or premium—which grade of gasoline should you run in your car? Advisors disagree on whether or not higher grades are worth the higher prices.

Once you own a car, calculating your actual fuel efficiency is simple. Step 1: Fill up the gas tank and note your current odometer reading. Step 2: Next time you fill up the gas tank, note how many gallons (or liters) it takes. Also note your new odometer reading. Step 3: Subtract the previous miles (or kilometers) from the current reading. Divide that number by the number of gallons (or liters) it took to refill the gasoline tank.

Example: You've driven 300 miles (482.7 km) since last filling your tank, and it takes 15 gallons (56.8 L) of gas to refill. Divide 300 by 15 (or 482.7 km by 56.8 L). You're getting 20 miles to a gallon (8.5 km to a liter) of gas. That's not good—either for your wallet or for the environment.

Much nicer example: You've driven 400 miles (643.6 km) and it takes 10 gallons (37.9 L) to refill your tank. Divide 400 by 10 (or 643.6 km by 37.9 L). You're getting 40 miles to a gallon (17 km to a liter) of gas!

Until you actually own the car and make those calculations repeatedly over time, you can't know exactly how fuel-efficient the car is going to be.

New or Used?

Some veteran consumers never buy used cars. Others always do. Their thinking runs something like the following:

New: "If I buy a new car and trade it in in two or three years (within its warranty period), I'm unlikely to ever face major repair expenses. If I follow this policy for the rest of my life, I'll always enjoy relatively new, problem-free cars."

One main drawback is that you'll be making car payments constantly for the rest of your life. If you can afford that, then it's basically a sound car-buying philosophy.

Used: "If I research carefully, I can buy a very good used car that's only a couple of years old, with low mileage (kilometrage), for much less than a new model of the same car. I'll enjoy it just as much as driving the newer model and pay much less—both for the purchase and for property taxes."

That may be a better idea than only going for the new. But you have to know exactly what you're buying (examine the car carefully and test-drive it). You also need to possess an instinct for when it's time to trade. Generally, repair costs will mount as a car ages. Buying an old car can be risky, and it may no longer be under warranty. Don't buy someone else's problems.

The Blue Book and Car Buying

You may have heard the term "blue book value" in car trading. The *Kelley Blue Book* has been a trusted automobile valuation resource for many years.

When it is time to buy, sell, or trade your car, it's good to know approximately how much it is worth at current market values. The Kelley Blue Book is the standard resource for valuing a new or used car. You can perform an online evaluation for free at www.kbb.com. Enter the car's year, make, model, odometer reading, estimated condition, and your zip code in the United States or postal code in Canada (where you live affects car values). Check off specific features. The *Blue Book* then shows you the car's trade-in value (the amount of discount you should expect to receive from a dealer if you trade it for another car), private party value (what the car is worth if it is bought or sold by private individuals), and suggested retail value (the price at which the car dealer will probably sell the car after trading with you).

Kelley's Perfect Car Finder is an internet tool that lets you search for car models by price range, vehicle type, category, manufacturer, seating capacity, estimated fuel economy, and size.

The Option of Leasing

Leasing seems to cost less per month than buying, if the advertisements are to be believed. And what a car you can get! It's not only new—it's a very nice car. Think executive level.

If you're an executive, a car lease might make sense. If you aren't an executive, think twice.

A leasing company will probably require a client to be twenty-one years old. You, the client, must buy insurance, perhaps more insurance than you would need if you actually owned the car. You are limited in the number of miles (kilometers) that you can drive in a year. If you go over, you pay extra. If you decide after a few months or a year that you don't like your lease agreement, it will cost you extra just to get out of it.

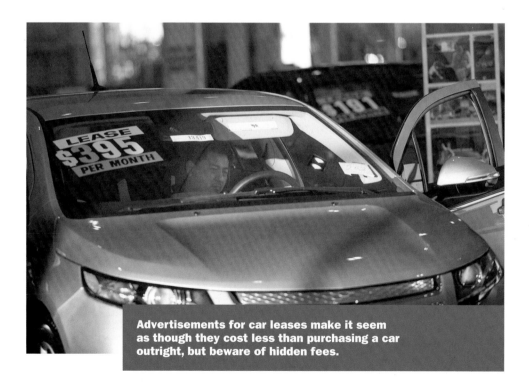

Advertisements for car leases make it seem as though they cost less than purchasing a car outright, but beware of hidden fees.

At the end of the lease period, you can turn in the car or buy it (usually not at a bargain price). If you don't buy it, then you own nothing. You have enjoyed day-to-day driving but have made no investment. A car owner, by contrast, still has a drivable, sellable product.

Do the Research

If you're a money-smart car shopper, you will spend many hours over a period of weeks or months reading car reviews and comparisons. Ask friends what they like and dislike about the cars that they drive. Visit auto dealerships in your area. If test-drives are allowed, take them. Constantly ask questions.

CHAPTER THREE

Wheeling and Dealing

What do you do once you have chosen the car you like and can afford? Now it's time to find out how to get it for the best possible price. You will need to think carefully about whether you want a monthly car payment. Though the payment might seem like a reasonable deal, the costs can be a lot higher than you realize.

Dealerships and You

Car dealers buy new cars from the manufacturer for a certain price and then sell them to customers at a higher price. That is how dealers earn a profit. The more they can get above what they pay the manufacturer, the higher their profit. Dealers want all customers to think that they've gotten a great deal, regardless of the price they negotiate.

The manufacturer charges its dealers what is called the invoice price. One way that dealers attract customers is to advertise that they are selling vehicles for only a fraction "above invoice" (the amount they paid the manufacturer) or even "below invoice." They can do this and still earn a profit because they often receive money back from manufacturers if certain car models are not selling well. The money that the automaker pays back to the dealer is called a rebate. In some instances, the manufacturer actually charges the dealer less than the manufacturer's own invoice price. This price reduction is called a discount.

Buyers can truly get deals on vehicles that haven't been selling. Bear in mind, though, that there are usually good reasons why few people want to buy them. Those models may have a poor maintenance record, they may get low fuel economy, or they may hold unusually low resale values.

Pay careful attention to the details of the different stickers. For example: The manufacturer's invoice lists all the costs that the dealer has paid to the manufacturer, including freight—the charge for transporting the car from the factory to the dealership (also known

Car dealerships have a variety of new and used, or preowned, vehicles to choose from.

as the destination or delivery charge). Some dealers have been known to add freight fees to their sticker prices. If you don't catch it, then you will pay twice for shipment.

It's wise to have an adult adviser with you when you negotiate to buy a car. Once you are pleased with the terms and the car is within your budget, some trading smarts might save you hundreds or even thousands of dollars. Never jump at the seller's first offer. If you truly believe you can get a better deal elsewhere, then tell the dealer.

When buying a used car, the original invoice price will mean little. What you want to know before sitting down to bargain with the seller is the car's blue book value. You also need to obtain as many details as you can about the history of the car. Was it wrecked? (If so, how many times? To what extent?) Was it

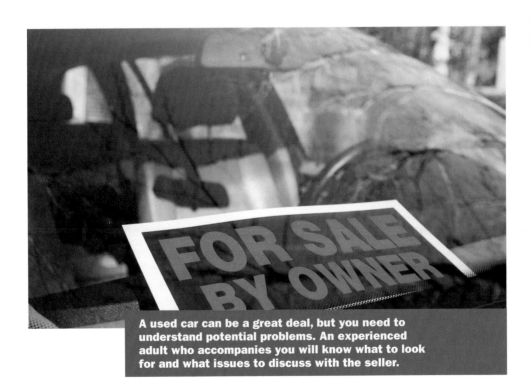

A used car can be a great deal, but you need to understand potential problems. An experienced adult who accompanies you will know what to look for and what issues to discuss with the seller.

washed over in a flood? Has it been repaired with cheap replacement parts? If so, then those nonfactory parts—especially in the emissions system—can damage related parts. Substandard replacement parts can make a warranty legally worthless.

Upkeep and Warranties

New cars and some used cars are sold under warranty. That means that if certain parts break or act up during the first few years of ownership, then the dealer or manufacturer must fix the car for free. Some warranties are more useful than others. Some fail to cover certain types of problems or parts. If a dealer promises bumper-to-bumper coverage, you would think that means the warranty will pay for anything that goes wrong with the car. But many so-called bumper-to-bumper warranties exclude some items.

Dealers frequently try to persuade customers to pay extra for an extended warranty or a separate service contract. This, they explain, will cover additional risks not covered under the manufacturer's standard warranty. It may add more time or driving miles (kilometers) to the life of the original warranty.

Some car dealers (including used car dealers) offer warranties for the "life" of the car, with "unlimited miles" and "unlimited time" for certain vehicles. Read the fine print. No seller is honestly willing to perform all future repairs at no charge until the wheels fall off the car. It's a sales device.

Time for a Loan

Ideally, the purchaser has enough money on hand to pay for the car in full. That requires years of careful savings. Most buyers must obtain a loan in order to purchase a car. This lets them pay

An extended warranty on a car may be a good idea in order to avoid paying for mechanical problems in the future.

for the car over a period of years, during which time they can use and enjoy the vehicle. Loans cost money. Depending on the terms of the loan, the person usually pays several thousand dollars more for the car than the negotiated price.

The buyer must pay at least a small amount of the agreed-upon price up front. This is called the down payment. (With later car purchases, the dealer may accept a trade-in vehicle as the down payment.) A bank or mortgage company will loan the buyer money to pay the remainder of the purchase cost. (Actually, the bank buys the car from the dealer. The customer then buys it from the bank.) Some car dealerships have their own lending companies.

The bank or finance company makes money by charging the customer interest on the loan. The customer eventually must pay the bank the purchase price plus the interest fee. Interest rates on

Getting Enough Coverage

A factory warranty may cover major repairs for the first three years or 50,000 miles (80,465 km), whichever is reached first. An extended warranty or service contract might lengthen coverage to the first six years or 100,000 miles (160,930 km). It might also promise to cover problems that are not included under the regular warranty.

Automotive experts and many consumers are leery of extended service contracts. They believe the extra coverage is not worth the cost. Car owners frequently discover that when a problem arises, the service contract doesn't cover it. Some contracts exclude certain types of repairs. They might require that the car owner pay the first $100, $200, $500, or even more of any repair fee. This means that for fairly inexpensive repairs, the owner has to pay the entire cost.

Before buying a service contract, read the fine print and ask questions. Make sure that you understand exactly what the agreement does and doesn't include.

car loans vary widely, from 1 or 2 percent to higher than 10 percent. Usually, the more money you can put down, the lower the interest rate you can get.

A computer amortization program can calculate the exact amount that you will have to pay back. The loan payback depends on three factors: 1) the amount of money borrowed after making

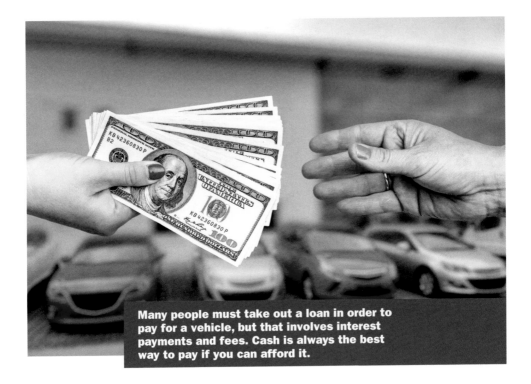

Many people must take out a loan in order to pay for a vehicle, but that involves interest payments and fees. Cash is always the best way to pay if you can afford it.

the down payment, 2) the annual percentage rate of the loan, and 3) the payback period.

As a simple example, suppose you agree to pay $18,000 for your car and you are able to give the dealer $3,000 down. That means you must borrow $15,000. You find a lending institution that will loan you that amount at an annual interest rate of 10 percent. Ten percent of $15,000 equals $1,500 per year.

The good news is that you must pay interest only on the on-going principal amount of the loan. With each monthly payment, you reduce the remaining principal amount. A portion of each payment is applied toward the principal; a smaller portion is interest. Every month, a slightly higher portion goes toward principal and a lower portion goes toward interest.

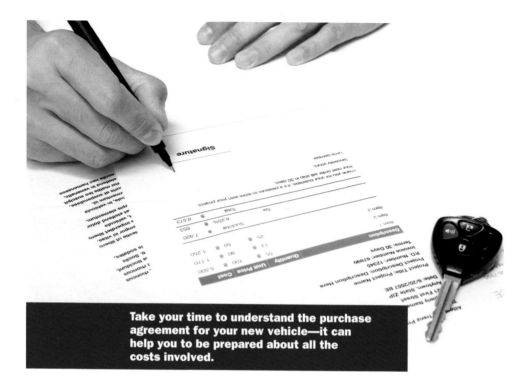

Take your time to understand the purchase agreement for your new vehicle—it can help you to be prepared about all the costs involved.

Obviously, the sooner you can pay off the loan, the less you will have to pay in interest. The only good reason to negotiate a longer loan period is that you'll have more easily affordable monthly payments. For most car buyers, the key decision is how much they can afford to pay for a car each month.

An amortization program reveals how much your monthly payments will be. It also shows, month by month, how much of your money is going to principal and how much to interest. It keeps track of the total amount you have paid in principal and interest at any given point during the loan period. At the end, you can see how much in interest the loan has cost you.

If you sign a $15,000 loan contract at a 10 percent interest rate and you commit to pay it off in three years, then your monthly payments will be about $484. At the end, you will have paid $2,424 in interest. That, added to the $18,000 purchase price (your $3,000 down, plus $15,000 borrowed), means the car has cost you $20,424.

If you take four years to pay off the car loan, then you will have to pay only $380 per month, but the total interest will be $3,023. The car will have cost you $21,023. If you take five years to pay off your loan, then your monthly payment comes down to about $319 and your total interest goes up to $3,380. The car will have cost you $21,380.

As you can see, you will save almost $1,000 if you can make the monthly payments for a three-year loan, rather than a five-year loan. You'll also be free of the burden of car payments two years sooner—a very nice relief, as longtime car owners well know. With most loans, you can pay extra in months when you have more money available. This might shorten the loan term and save some of the interest costs.

It's hard for a high school student to qualify for a car loan, even a student who has a part-time job. You may need your parents to obtain the loan for you. They may expect you to make the full monthly payments or a big part.

One final tip: If a car dealer requires you to take out a loan through its in-house or preferred lending institution, walk away from the deal. Many other banks and credit unions are available.

CHAPTER **FOUR**

Powering Up

I n fall 1973, America faced an unexpected fuel shortage. Suddenly, the gas that Americans had come to depend on for transportation was not available, at least in the amounts that everyone needed. What was available soared in costs.

What caused the fuel crisis was a brief war in the Middle East. Israel, a Jewish nation, was fighting against two Muslim nations, Egypt and Syria. The Organization of Petroleum Exporting Countries (OPEC) is a league of fifteen oil-producing nations, most of them Muslim countries. OPEC voted to stop exporting oil to Western countries that supported Israel. Within days, gas stations in the United States and other countries began running out of gas. Cars and trucks lined up at the stations that did have gas. Station owners began rationing their supplies, limiting customers to only $5 or $10 worth of gas at a time. Other rationing systems were devised. In some areas, drivers could buy gas only on odd or even days, determined by their license plate numbers.

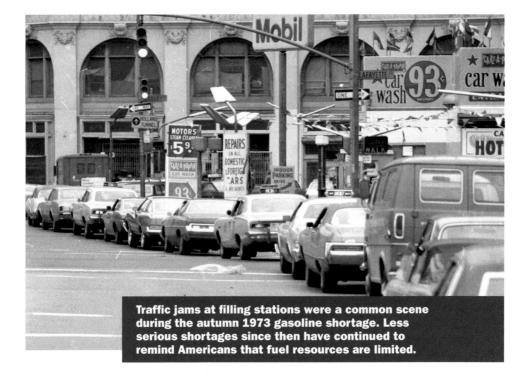

Traffic jams at filling stations were a common scene during the autumn 1973 gasoline shortage. Less serious shortages since then have continued to remind Americans that fuel resources are limited.

The good thing about the 1973 fuel crisis was that it made drivers think about energy and ways to conserve gasoline. Sadly, after the crisis passed, most drivers went back to their old, wasteful consumption of gasoline.

The United States has not experienced another energy shortage that serious since. There have been local and regional gas shortages, though. Gas shortages occurred in advance of Hurricane Florence in September 2018. States in the path of the hurricane, such as North Carolina, ran out of gas because people who had evacuated ahead of the storm filled up their tanks, as did people who made the decision to stay despite official's warnings.

Natural disasters, wars that affect gasoline supplies, and environmental awareness have led many people to seek alternative forms of transportation. The use of fossil fuels, including gasoline, contributes to pollution. Consumers are interested in fuel types that are not subject to unpredictable, faraway developments. They are also interested in power sources that will cause less damage to the environment.

Gas for Getting Around

The great majority of cars are fueled by gasoline. Auto engineers, scientists, government officials, consumer groups, and experimental individuals endeavor to find better alternatives. For the near future, however, most of your choices will be gas-powered autos.

If you buy a gas-powered car, then you become the typical customer at the pump. Your car budget will be affected by price trends and crises in petroleum production and supply. When prices rise or when supplies are limited, you can only grumble and bear it—and look for ways to conserve on gas.

One pump choice you do have is the fuel grade you will use. When you pull up to a gas pump, you will find at least two, usually three, choices: regular, midgrade, and premium. The differences in price are about 10 cents per gallon (13 cents per liter). What is the advantage of paying more for higher gasoline grades?

Most cars run fine on the cheapest grade, regular. Some cars, such as sports cars, have engines that function best on higher gas grades. These are called high-performance cars.

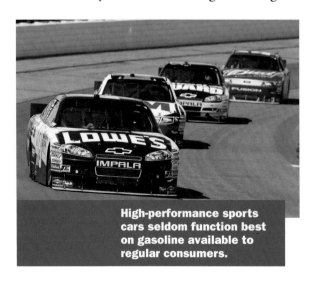

High-performance sports cars seldom function best on gasoline available to regular consumers.

They will run on regular gasoline, but their engines might begin to knock or "ping." Some advisers say the engine noise is barely noticeable and is basically harmless. Others say using the wrong gas grade can damage an engine. A good rule of thumb is to read consumer accounts and ask the car dealer.

Saving Money on Gas

Even after you buy your car, don't drive if you can walk or bike instead. This advice applies with any car you buy, regardless of its power supply or fuel/mileage economy rating.

Carpool whenever possible. Share a ride to that distant concert or sports event with friends. (It would be nice if they would buy the gas, since you're providing the car.)

Combine errands. When you can, combine business with pleasure, too. If you would like to check out the new seasonal clothes at the mall and you have library books due, and the library is between your home and the mall, make one trip. If you want to make a bank deposit and your bank is on the way to your job, stop by the bank on your way to or from work.

Remember that the faster you drive, the more gas you consume.

Reasons to Limit Driving

It's wonderful to have your own car! You're proud and free. Financial experts, though, put a damper on the excitement. They advise that you drive it only when necessary.

First-time car owners have a hard time abiding by that. They've already planned fun trips. They want to show off their "wheels" to friends. They would like to drive around the town and countryside, enjoying the special scent of a new car's interior and the feeling of power.

It's OK to enjoy your car, but money-smart drivers understand the need for discipline. They always count the cost in advance. If you want to drive to an event that is in a distant city,

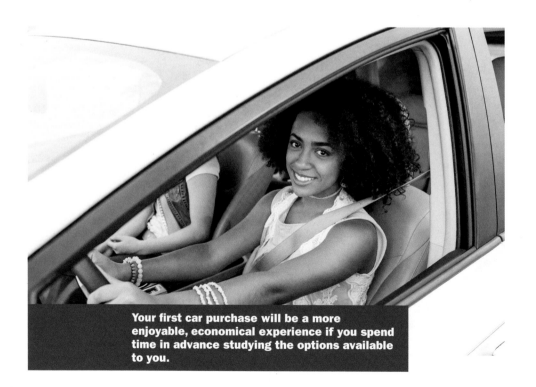

Your first car purchase will be a more enjoyable, economical experience if you spend time in advance studying the options available to you.

calculate the round-trip mileage (kilometrage). Depending on your car's fuel economy and current pump prices, a 100-mile (160 km) trip could cost you $20 to $30 just for the gasoline.

Other Kinds of Fuel

Gas-powered vehicles are the most common. There are two major reasons to consider buying a car powered by a different fuel type.

First, fossil fuels like petroleum (the source of our gas and oil) won't last forever. They were made naturally over a period of millions of years. They came from the earth, and the supply is limited. When they are all used up, that will be the end of the fossil fuel story. Scientists can only speculate how much more

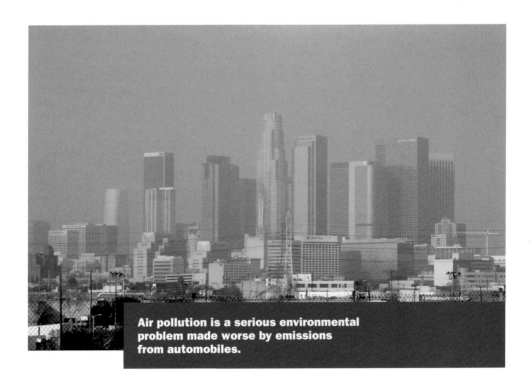

Air pollution is a serious environmental problem made worse by emissions from automobiles.

fossil fuel is available. The supply will probably last longer than your lifetime, but it will be gone eventually.

Second, the burning of fossil fuels produces carbon dioxide and badly pollutes the earth's atmosphere. Experimenters have proven that other types of automotive power cause less atmospheric damage—practically no damage, in some cases.

Money is a factor. In general, cars that run with alternative energy are more expensive. The purchase price almost certainly will be higher than that for a gas-powered vehicle. After the purchase, the fuel/energy supply may or may not cost you more to keep the car on the road. You can find out many of the details by researching in advance. You should ask the car seller about the long-term economics of the deal.

You might conclude that it's important to invest in an alternative-powered car for the sake of the environment, even if it costs more. You may decide to buy a gas-powered car that gets excellent fuel efficiency and produces a low level of hazardous emissions. Unavoidably, some people need a vehicle type (perhaps a five-passenger, four-wheel-drive truck) that simply can't meet economic or environmental ideals.

Alternative power systems include the following:

Diesel. Diesel engines and special diesel fuel have been used since the early 1900s, notably by the military and the trucking industry. Modern diesel fuel is a petroleum (fossil fuel) product, but it costs less to produce than standard gasoline does. It has several other advantages, too. Besides being safer to handle than gasoline, it contains less sulfur, making it less polluting. For money watchers, its main asset is that diesel engines get roughly a third better fuel efficiency than gas-powered engines.

Biodiesel. Scientists have found that more environmentally friendly, biologically grown fuels can be blended with traditional diesel fuel. Soybean oil is an example. Some forms of biodiesel fuel can reduce harmful exhaust by as much as two-thirds, compared to pure gasoline.

Ethanol. This is a type of alcohol brewed not for human consumption but for powering cars. It can be produced from corn and other biological ingredients, including certain waste materials.

Electric. Electric cars are available in the United States. Specialty shops can convert some gas-powered

Electric cars can reduce pollutants in the air, but they have disadvantages as well. For example, they often have limited ranges.

automobiles to electric power by adding batteries. Certain car designs are easier to convert than others. A major problem with electric cars is limited range. You can't drive nearly as far on an electrical battery charge as you can on a tank of gasoline. For short daily trips, though, this may be an option worth considering. You may have to recharge the battery only once every few days. Keep in mind that electrical current costs money, too.

Hybrid. A hybrid is an electrically powered vehicle that also has a gas or diesel engine. Why? The purpose of the petroleum-based system is to keep the electric batteries charged. This helps solve the problem of limited range.

Other alternatives. Natural gas can power cars efficiently. However, like , it is an earth-bound natural resource. Sooner or later, the world's supply of natural gas will be gone. Another energy source is hydrogen, but the cost of researching, developing, and marketing it is high.

If you are interested in investing in an alternatively powered vehicle, then make sure that you understand all the costs, both short term and long term, before you buy. It may cost you more to purchase but save you more in the long run—or it may cost more altogether. In some instances, it comes down to a decision between car economy and environmental responsibility.

CHAPTER **FIVE**

Keep It or Sell It?

Most people find that it is smart to keep a car as long as possible after it's paid for. The cost of owning a car becomes much more affordable without monthly loan payments. However, as the vehicle ages and requires more repairs, you could find yourself paying more to keep the old car running than a sizable down payment on a new car.

Some people trade cars every two or three years. (A few trade every year.) The main advantage for these people—apart from always having a nice, new car—is that with a newer car, they're more likely to avoid the cost of major repairs.

The disadvantage is that the quick seller takes a beating on the buy/sell exchange. A car begins losing its value the moment you buy it. If you buy a new car for $20,000 and trade it three years later, then you might be offered no more than $10,000 for it—half your purchase price. Did you get your money's worth

Mounting repair costs signal that it's time to trade your vehicle in for a different one. Your mechanic may be able to advise you on the longevity of your vehicle.

during that brief time? If you keep it for another three years, then the resale value might be reduced to $5,000. As you can see, it lost $10,000 in resale value during the first three years but only $5,000 more during the next three years. If you keep the car for ten years or longer, then you might receive only $1,000 for it when you finally trade. However, you'll have gotten ten years of drive time.

A car loses resale value rapidly during the first few years. Later, the rate of decreasing value levels off. The longer you keep it, the more value you will get from it.

Lemon Laws

A car that has a recurring problem is called a lemon. All US states have lemon laws. They require automakers to replace or buy back cars that, after repeated attempts, have not been repaired satisfactorily under terms of the warranty. If you have repeated problems with your new car and the dealer is unhelpful, then you may have a case under your state's lemon law. What about used lemons? They may not be as easy to challenge under your state's lemon law. To what extent are you protected, then, under state law? You should find out your legal options before buying a used car.

Keeping Your Car in Good Shape

No matter how long you plan to keep your car, keep it in good shape. Regular maintenance will help your car last longer and avoid major repairs as it ages. It will also help keep the car's resale value as high as possible.

Repairs are inevitable. They might be as simple and inexpensive as having a punctured tire patched for $10 to $20. If the tire cannot be repaired, then a new tire might cost $50 to $200. That's minor, though, compared with major car repairs. Structural and engine repairs can easily run into thousands of dollars. When faced with a repair estimate of $3,000 or more on a car with an

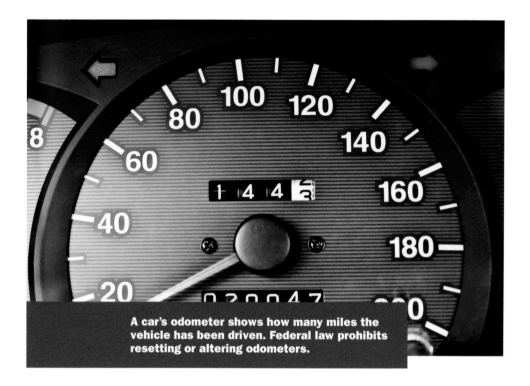

A car's odometer shows how many miles the vehicle has been driven. Federal law prohibits resetting or altering odometers.

estimated blue book value of perhaps $1,000, you have to ask yourself, "Should I keep this car?"

Meanwhile, keep the odometer in mind. The odometer reading will greatly affect your car's resale value.

No matter how well you maintain your car and how low you keep the mileage (kilometrage), the car will depreciate, or decrease in value, simply because it is getting old. When it's time to sell or trade your car, you should find out approximately how much it is worth. For used car sellers and buyers alike, the *Kelley Blue Book* is the standard pricing guide.

10 Great Questions to Ask a Car Dealer

1. According to my budget, I can afford the monthly payments you're estimating for this car. I can also afford fuel, regular maintenance checkups, and insurance. What other expenses am I overlooking?

2. If I'll need a parent to help me obtain the car loan, and I make the payments, will the car belong to my parent or to me after it's paid for?

3. I'm interested in leasing as well as in buying a car. Am I old enough to lease?

4. Are used cars that have been leased or driven in company fleets usually good buys?

5. You're asking much more for this used car than the Blue Book suggested price. Why?

6. Before I buy this new car, can you tell me how rapidly it's likely to decrease in value in the coming years, assuming ordinary wear?

7. Does your advertised price include sales tax?

8. How often will I need to bring in the car for servicing? What's the average maintenance charge?

9. How much should I expect to pay for a new set of tires? How many miles should I expect to get from new tires?

10. Rather than trading my old car for this new one, I'm thinking of selling the old one myself. Would it be to my advantage to trade it with you?

CHAPTER SIX

Alternative Cars and Vehicles

There's one very good reason to get a vehicle that uses less or no gas: the environment. The fewer pollutants released into the air, the better for all of us. Gasoline is a big polluter worldwide. Why not avoid contributing to environmental problems as much as possible?

The following are some car-alternative options that you might want to think about. All of them will save you gas money. But be aware that all of them also pose safety risks. These vehicles are much smaller than what you normally encounter on the highway. Whenever they're involved in accidents, they almost always receive worse damage than larger vehicles.

Small "Smart" Cars

You've probably seen them: little two-seat "bug" cars. If you've seen them on an interstate highway with an eighteen-wheel truck bearing down on their bumper at 70 miles per hour (113 kmh), then you probably have decided that you don't want to be inside one of them.

But they serve a purpose. To rove high-speed interstate high-ways? Probably not. But to get around town or take jaunts on quiet back roads? Perhaps.

Smart cars have many definitions. Some call them superminis or microcars. They are also lovingly called smart-ies. They can go up to

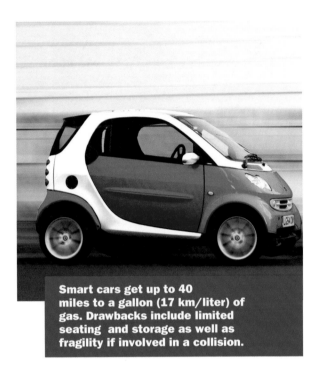

Smart cars get up to 40 miles to a gallon (17 km/liter) of gas. Drawbacks include limited seating and storage as well as fragility if involved in a collision.

80 miles per hour (130 kmh). Prices and locations vary. They may cost as little as $12,000 or as much as $30,000, depending on the features they include. Some smart cars are electric, boasting a range of up to 100 miles (161 km) between charges.

Many observers believe smart cars are better suited for Euro-peans, who need to drive shorter distances than Americans do. But Americans are beginning to take notice. Some are thinking that a smart car is just the kind of car they need. But smart cars are comparatively rare in the United States. You may have to get on a waiting list to buy a new one. Used smart cars are sold locally and through online auctions.

Although they are turning heads and are environmentally friendly, smart cars are not much more economical than many late-model compact cars. They can get up to 40 miles per gallon (17 km per liter) of gas.

Considering Pros and Cons

People interested in buying an alternative vehicle are attracted mainly by its economy. They also like that it pollutes the atmosphere less than conventional vehicles do. They may be impressed by the visual appeal—the "cute" look of a smart car or scooter or the exciting designs of late-model motorcycles.

The obvious factor that turns other buyers away is the size. Only one passenger besides the driver can ride on a scooter or motorcycle or inside a smart car, and few items can be carried along. Another negative is the lack of comfort compared to roomier vehicles. Finally, maintenance is inconvenient if the nearest service shop is across town or in a distant city.

Motorcycles and More

You will need a special driver's license or permit and substantial experience in order to drive a motorcycle or scooter. Motorcycle laws vary among states, in terms of vehicle classes and age requirements. (Although some states don't require it, do wear a helmet.) You can buy a new motorcycle for less than $10,000 and a good used one for around $5,000. Fuel economy? Expect to get 50 to 60 miles to a gallon (21.25–25.5 km per liter) of gas.

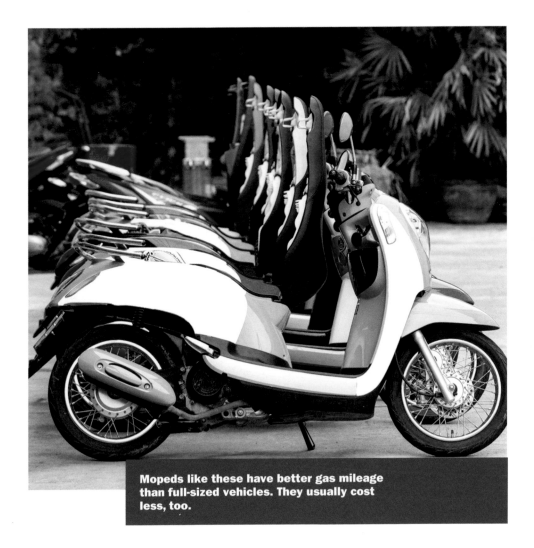

Mopeds like these have better gas mileage than full-sized vehicles. They usually cost less, too.

You can drive 80 or 90 miles per hour (129–145 kmh) on a motorcycle if you want to flirt with death.

A motor scooter with a 150cc (cubic centimeter) engine can move you around at 60 miles per hour (97 kmh) or faster at an economy rating of about 80 miles per gallon (34 km per liter) of gasoline. The purchase price is under $1,500 for many Chinese-built models and more for American- and European-made scooters. You can buy scooters with 250cc or larger engines. Generally, the larger the engine, the faster you can go but the lower your gas mileage (kilometrage) will be. Some scooters can press 100 miles per hour (160 kmh), but don't expect remarkable fuel economy. And you really would be risking your life at that speed on a scooter. Scooters are designed for fairly short-distance, moderate-speed driving. Motorcycles are more controllable than scooters at higher speeds.

A moped with a 50cc engine or smaller can go only about 35 miles per hour (56 kmh) but can carry you more than 100 miles on a gallon (42.5 km per liter) of gas. Some high school and college students have decided that a moped is just what they need for their day-to-day transportation. You can buy a new moped for under $1,000. In many states, you don't need a motorcycle permit, license tag, or special insurance to own and drive it. But you do have to be the state's required age and pass a driver's test.

Motorcycle and scooter maintenance costs less than car maintenance does. For example, whereas an oil change for a car may require 4 quarts (3.8 L) of new oil, a two-wheel vehicle may require a quart (just under 1 L) or less.

But maintenance is a thorny issue for two-wheel motorists in some locations. It's simple to arrange an inexpensive car tune-up within easy driving distance of your home. Cycle and scooter service centers, by contrast, are not as easy to find. Many two-wheel drivers learn to do their own maintenance. This can save them lots of money if they're willing to master the details and perform the work. A do-it-yourself, two-wheel owner must be diligent in maintaining the engine, transmission, tires, brakes, battery, shock absorbers, and other parts for safety reasons.

Safety is a major factor to consider when you purchase a small vehicle. Be sure to wear protective gear to minimize injuries from accidents.

Safety and the Alternative Vehicle

It definitely is not safe if you do not know how to drive your two-wheeler or maneuver your smart car among larger vehicles in thick traffic. Highway department officials lay it out in plain language: if you are a driver or passenger aboard a cycle or inside a microsize car and you're involved in a collision, then you almost always will get the worst of it. The other vehicle might be a truck, an SUV, or an eighteen-wheeler.

That does not necessarily mean you should avoid alternative vehicles. It just means you must plan and understand your transportation needs very carefully. Where do you need to drive? How far? How often? Do you need a versatile first car—one that can

take you around the block and carry you on long-distance jour-
neys? Will you be jostling frequently with interstate traffic?

Smart cars are considered urban vehicles, to be driven around
the city or on short trips. So are scooters. Mopeds are not intend-
ed to be driven more than a few miles at a time. Motorcycles, on
the other hand, may be long-distance cruisers.

Responsibility and Owning a Car

Whether you buy a new car, used car, small car, big car, gas-
powered or alternate car, or a two-wheel vehicle, you must do
your homework in advance. Understand all of the costs, not just
the purchase price. Be prepared to deal with unexpected expenses.
Make sure that you can afford not only to buy the car but also to
keep it running.

Always be mindful of ways to conserve. Transportation is often a luxury, not a necessity. The less you drive, the better off the
environment will be—and the better off your budget will be.

GLOSSARY

amortization program A computer program that calculates details of a loan.

cabriolet A two-door convertible with a small backseat.

consumer A buyer or user of a product.

deductible An amount of an insurance claim that the insured person must pay before the insurance company begins its coverage.

depreciate To lose value; except for classic vehicles, all cars depreciate over time.

discount A lowering of the stated price of an item.

down payment The amount of money a car buyer pays in cash (or by check) before taking out a loan for the remainder of the cost.

export To sell a product (such as oil) to buyers in other countries.

fossil fuel Petroleum, coal, or another type of fuel that was formed in the earth from plant or animal fossils over a long period of time.

hatchback A compact or subcompact car with a rear door that opens upward.

interest A percentage of a borrowed amount of money that must be paid to the lender or investor, in addition to the original amount.

invoice price The price that a car manufacturer charges its dealers.

kilometrage The total distance in kilometers.

maintenance Upkeep of a car.

MPV Multipurpose vehicle.

odometer The dashboard instrument that records how many miles (or kilometers) a car is driven.

optional equipment Additional features that a car buyer can purchase, such as power locks, cruise control, a built-in navigational system, etc.

petroleum Flammable oil used to prepare gasoline and other products.

principal The amount of money borrowed, not including interest.

rationing A system that forces people to use products like gasoline or food sparingly.

rebate Payback of part of a purchase price to the buyer.

sedan An average-size car with a backseat and either two or four doors.

sticker price The actual asking price on a car.

SUV Sport utility vehicle.

warranty The guarantee that if certain parts of a car do not work properly, they will be repaired or replaced at no cost to the buyer.

FOR MORE INFORMATION

American Automobile Association, Inc. (AAA)
607 14th Street NW #200
Washington, DC 20005
(202) 942-2050
Website: http://www.aaa.com
Facebook: @AAAFanPage
Twitter: @aaanews
AAA is a federation of automobile clubs across the United
States and in other countries. Besides member
services, it provides consumer information like new
and used car-buying tips.

Canada Extra
Consumers Union
101 Truman Avenue
Yonkers, NY 10703-1057
(914) 378-2000
Website: http://www.consumerreports.org/cro
/canadaextra/index.htm
Facebook, Twitter, and Instagram: @ConsumerReports
At Canada Extra, you can find Canada-specific information
about cars and other products provided by
ConsumerReports.org.

CARFAX
Website: http://www.carfax.com
Facebook: @carfax

Twitter: @carfaxreports

To aid used-car buyers, CARFAX, a commercial website, offers vehicle history information on car and light truck models made since 1981. Its databases reportedly contain information on more than five billion vehicles, identifying them by their vehicle identification numbers (VINs).

Cars.com
Classified Ventures, LLC
175 W. Jackson Boulevard
Chicago, IL 60604
(312) 601-5000
Website: http://www.cars.com
Facebook, Twitter, and Instagram: @CarsDotCom

This commercial website provides information from experts and consumers to help buyers formulate opinions on what to buy, where to buy, and how much to pay for a car.

ConsumerReports.org
Consumers Union
101 Truman Avenue
Yonkers, NY 10703-1057
(800) 333-0663
Website: http://www.consumerreports.org
Facebook, Twitter, and Instagram: @ConsumerReports

Consumer Reports publishes information for consumers about thousands of products, including new and used car models. It reports on cars by type: convertibles, small cars, minivans, pickups, SUVs, sedans, wagons, and sports cars.

Council of Better Business Bureaus
4200 Wilson Boulevard, Suite 800
Arlington, VA 22203-1838
(703) 276-0100
Website: http://www.bbb.org
Facebook: @BetterBusinessBureau
The council's auto-related consumer services include
buying tips and BBB AUTO LINE for resolving
warranty disputes.

Edmunds.com
Website: http://www.edmunds.com
Facebook and Twitter: @edmunds
Instagram: @edmundsdotcom
Edmunds, Inc., has been publishing new and used
automobile pricing guidelines since 1966.

Federal Trade Commission (FTC)
600 Pennsylvania Avenue NW
Washington, DC 20580
(202) 326-2222
Website: http://www.ftc.gov
Facebook: @federaltradecommission
Twitter: @FTC
The consumer information section of the FTC's website
includes advice on car purchasing, leasing, and
renting, as well as financing and maintenance.

Financial Planning Standards Council (FPSC)
902–375 University Avenue
Toronto, ON M5G 2J5
Canada

(800) 305-9886

Email: inform@fpsc.ca

Website: http://www.fpsc.ca

Facebook: @FPSC.Canada

Twitter: @FPSC_Canada

FPSC provides tailored information on personal finance, budgeting, savings, investments, and more for teens.

Kelley Blue Book Co., Inc.

195 Technology

Irvine, CA 92618

(800) 258-3266

Website: http://www.kbb.com

Facebook: @KBB

Twitter: @kelleybluebook

Long famous for its auto valuation service, the Kelley organization also provides online advice, reviews, and other material for car buyers and sellers.

National Automobile Dealers Association

8400 Westpark Drive

McLean, VA 22102

(800) 557-6232

Website: http://www.nada.org

Facebook and Twitter: @NADAUpdate

Instagram: @nada

This association puts on regional events for car dealers and holds them to certain standards. See especially the association's "Auto Financing Resources" page.

FOR FURTHER READING

Blohm, Craig E. *Teen Guide to Credit and Debt.* San Diego, CA: ReferencePoint Press, Inc., 2017.

Hardyman, Robyn. *Understanding Buying and Spending.* New York, NY: Rosen Publishing, 2018.

Hardyman, Robyn. *Understanding Money Goals and Budgeting.* New York, NY: Rosen Publishing, 2018.

Harmon, Daniel. *Smart Strategies for Buying a Car.* New York, NY: Rosen Publishing, 2015.

Marsico, Katie. *Using Credit Wisely.* Ann Arbor, MI: Cherry Lake Publishing, 2016.

McGuire, Kara. *Making Money Work: The Teens' Guide To Saving, Investing, and Building Wealth.* North Mankato, MN: Capstone Young Readers, 2015.

McGuire, Kara. *The Teen Money Manual: A Guide to Cash, Credit, Spending, Saving, Work, Wealth, and More.* North Mankato, MN: Capstone Young Readers, 2015.

Minden, Cecelia. *Living on a Budget.* Ann Arbor, MI: Cherry Lake Publishing, 2016.

Nagle, Jeanne. *Money, Banking, and Finance.* New York, NY: Rosen Publishing, 2018.

Schlesinger, Emily, and Jennifer Liss. *Managing Money.* Costa Mesa, CA: Saddleback Educational Publishing, 2017.

Uhl, Xina M., and Judy Monroe Peterson. *Making a Budget.* New York, NY: Rosen Publishing, 2020.

Weeks, Marcus, and Derek Braddon. *Heads Up Money.* New York, NY: DK Publishing, 2016.

BIBLIOGRAPHY

Babej, Marc E., and Tim Pollak. "Is Smart a Dumb Idea?" *Forbes*, July 12, 2006. http://www.forbes .com/2006/07/12/unsolicited-advice-advertising -meb_0712smart.html.

Coppolla, Gabrielle. "Americans' Love Affair With Cars." *Bloomberg*, February 13, 2018. https://www .bloomberg.com/news/articles/2018-02-13 /americans-love-affair-with-cars.

Federal Trade Commission. "Buying a New Car." Facts for Consumers, November 2012. https://www .consumer.ftc.gov/articles/0209-buying-new-car.

Teens Guide to Money. "First Time Car Buying Tips for Teens." Retrieved on November 19, 2018. http:// www.teensguidetomoney.com/spending/first-time -car-buying-tips-for-teens/.

Kelley Blue Book. "10 Steps to Buying a New Car." Retrieved on November 19, 2018. https://www .kbb.com/car-advice/car-buying/step-1-know-your -shopping-style.

Kelley Blue Book. "10 Steps to Selling Your Car." Retrieved on November 19, 2018. https://www .kbb.com/sell-your-car/steps-to-sell-your-car.

Peters, Craig. "Mo-peds and Scooters Create a Debate on Wheels." GoUpstate.com, October 19, 2008. http://www.goupstate.com/news/20081019 /mo-peds-and-scooters-create-a-debate-on-wheels.

SmartCarOfAmerica.com. "Want to Buy a Smart Car?"
    Retrieved on November 19, 2018. https://www
    .smartcarofamerica.com/forums/f166/want-buy
    -smart-car-34571.

Straight Dope. "What's the Difference Between Premium
    and Regular Gas?" October 4, 2004. http://www
    .straightdope.com/columns/read/2565/whats-the
    -difference-between-premium-and-regular-gas.

Valdes-Dapena, Peter. "Invoice Price: What's It Really
    Worth?" CNNMoney.com, July 22, 2004. http://
    money.cnn.com/2003/11/24/pf/autos/invoice
    _price/index.htm.

Woodyard, Chris. "America Crazy About Breadbox on
    Wheels Called Smart Car." *USA Today*, November 12,
    2007. http://www.usatoday.com/money
    /autos/2007-11-11-smartcar_N.htm.

INDEX

ABOUT THE AUTHORS

Xina M. Uhl has authored a variety of books for young people in addition to textbooks, teacher's guides, lessons, and assessment questions. When she is not writing or reading, she enjoys travel, photography, and hiking with her dogs. Her blog features her travel adventures and latest fiction projects.

Daniel E. Harmon was the author of many books and numerous articles for national and regional magazines and newspapers. In high school, he drove an aging, imported lemon, whenever it decided to start up and move. When he entered college, his mother found a terrific deal on a used compact sedan; he worked part time and shared college and car expenses with his parents. He bought a 150cc motor scooter for daily errands and calculated that he saved 10 cents every mile he used the scooter instead of the car. He lived in Spartanburg, South Carolina.

PHOTO CREDITS

Cover BFG Images/Getty Images; cover, p. 1 (wallet logo) logomills/Shutterstock.com; p. 5 Barry Austin Photography/Photodisc/Getty Images; p. 8 fotog/Getty Images; p. 9 © iStockphoto.com/NoDerog; p. 10 Radius Images/Getty Images; p. 12 Patti McConville/Alamy Stock Photo; p. 16 Przemyslaw Klos/EyeEm/Getty Images; p. 17 betto Rodrigues/Shutterstock.com; p. 18 Melinda Fawver/Shutterstock.com; p. 21 Bloomberg/Getty Images; p. 24 David McNew/Getty Images; p. 25 Martin Diebel/Getty Images; p. 27 Rob Orf/Shutterstock.com; p. 29 RomanR/Shutterstock.com; p. 30 ST22Studio/Shutterstock.com; p. 33 New York Daily News Archive/Getty Images; p. 34 Action Sports Photography/Shutterstock.com; p. 36 kali9/E+/Getty Images; p. 37 mikeledray/Shutterstock.com; p. 39 Tom Uhlman/Alamy Stock Photo; p. 42 4 PM production/Shutterstock.com; p. 44 PaulPaladin/Shutterstock.com; p. 47 ben smith/Shutterstock.com; p. 49 CharlotteRaboff/Shutterstock.com; p. 51 Canetti/Shutterstock.com.

Design: Raúl Rodriguez, R studio T, NYC;
Layout: Tahara Anderson; Photo Researcher: Sherri Jackson